A Beginner's Guide to Passive Funds (ETF)

The Right Information for Financial Freedom

NICOLAS LEONARD

© Copyright 2020 by Nicolas Lèonard. All right reserved.

The work contained herein has been produced with the intent to provide relevant knowledge and information on the topic on the topic described in the title for entertainment purposes only. While the author has gone to every extent to furnish up to date and true information, no claims can be made as to its accuracy or validity as the author has made no claims to be an expert on this topic. Notwithstanding, the reader is asked to do their own research and consult any subject matter experts they deem necessary to ensure the quality and accuracy of the material presented herein.

This statement is legally binding as deemed by the Committee of Publishers Association and the American Bar Association for the territory of the United States. Other jurisdictions may apply their own legal statutes. Any reproduction, transmission, or copying of this material contained in this work without the express written consent of the copyright holder shall be deemed as a copyright violation as per the current legislation in force on the date of publishing and subsequent time thereafter. All additional works derived from this material may be claimed by the holder of this copyright.

The data, depictions, events, descriptions and all other information forthwith are considered to be true, fair, and accurate unless the work is expressly described as a work of fiction. Regardless of the nature of this work, the Publisher is exempt from any responsibility of actions taken by the reader in conjunction with this work. The Publisher acknowledges that the reader acts of their own accord and releases the author and Publisher of any responsibility for the observance of tips, advice, counsel, strategies and techniques that may be offered in this volume.

Table of Contents

Introduction

Chapter 1: Changing Your Mindset
Learning to Take Risks
Shifting the Money Mindset
Money Is Not Evil
The Law of Attraction
Investing Basics

Chapter 2: Understanding the Other Side
Inflation
Big Banks
Promoters
Your Biggest Opponent

Chapter 3: Passive Investment Funds
Active Investing
Passive Funds Pros and Cons
Index Fund Categories
ETFs Versus Mutual Funds
Precious Metals
Bear Market and Bull Market
Stocks, Bonds, and Liquid Assets
Hiring a Financial Planner

Chapter 4: Learning to Save
Creating A Budget
Keeping Your Money Safe
Different Financial Institutions:
InsuranceIt's Simple Math

Chapter 5: The Time Advantage
The Benefits of Starting Early
Knowing When You're Ready
Long-Term Investing
Starting Late

Chapter 6: The Miracle of Compound Interest
Investment Accounts for Earning Compound Interest
The Ugly Side

Chapter 7: Portfolio Models
Model Portfolio Examples
Steps to Building a Profitable Portfolio
Protecting Your Portfolio

Conclusion

Introduction

Congratulations on purchasing *A Beginner's Guide to Passive Funds,* and thank you for doing so. Money is a fascinating topic in life. It is something we are encouraged not to discuss, yet we are fascinated by it. In many cases, we worship it. We create our opinions of people based on their economic stature in life. The more money people make, the more respectable they are. This mindset is deep-rooted in various cultures around the world, and in order to determine where it comes from, we would have to delve into so many different factors. Honestly, it would take a whole other book or two to discuss it. For some people, money is everything. For others, it matters very little, if even at all.

Whatever your opinion on money may be, it cannot be denied that it is a major part of our lives. It is what drives decisions, policies, industry, households, and entertainment, among other things. Essentially, the old cliché of "money makes the world go around" is true in many aspects. Even if you don't care about money, it is a necessity for your life in some way. This being said, we must have a knowledge of money and finances in order to have a modicum of control in our lives. As adults, if we are financially dependent on someone, then they also have a certain amount of control over us.

Many of us have been indoctrinated with traditional money management techniques. These include: Find a good job that makes you money, save every penny you can, put away for retirement, do not spend what you do not have, and don't buy what you do not need. There is also the idea of earning your money the hard way through work and patience. These are good, safe practices, that can certainly create a nice nest egg for you. However, the mindset that creates these ideas is also limiting.

Many of the archaic ideas surrounding money have existed throughout the years and decades. However, as we learn more about finances and the different ways money can work, we learn new methods of creating wealth in our lives. A recent phenomenon that has taken over the world is the idea of passive funds. This is a major market strategy that we will discuss in this book. These funds, along with the market, in general, can be complicated at times, and if you are not paying close attention, it can be devastating to your finances in the long run. It is important to educate yourself and become informed before delving in. Once you do this, you may find that it is not as confusing as one would think. However, you can judge this for yourself.

Unfortunately, many people still have an archaic way of thinking when it comes to money. They do not realize that when it comes to finances, things are vastly different then they were during generations past. People must grow and evolve with the financial times in order to take advantage of the money that's out there. We hope to start shifting your way of thinking about money and open a whole new world for you.

The following chapters will discuss the importance of changing and constantly updating our financial mentality. In order to understand passive funds, we must change some of the traditional mindsets about money that we grew up with. Passive funds are a fascinating way to manage finances, and we will discuss exactly what these funds are, the benefits that come along with them, and what you need to look out for. There are many factors that can control the market, and if you cannot control them, you have to at least be aware of them. Finally, we will go over what portfolio models are and how they can benefit your personal finances for the rest of your life.

If you are someone who was educated on some of these nontraditional financial methods, then you will be familiar with many of the topics we discuss. However, there is still much you can learn based on different aspects of looking at passive funds. You can never know everything about a subject, and the goal of this book is to provide knowledge that is not very well-known to the general public. This includes people who are well-versed in the financial game. It is time to take control of your wealth, and engaging in passive funds is one way to do so. Learning to invest is essential, whether you want to create abundance or simply manage your finances better. Through this book, we will help get you informed.

One thing we will not do is give specific financial advice. We will also not promote any one company over another. We will simply provide you with the knowledge so you can ultimately make the best decision for yourself.

There are lots of books available on this topic; I really appreciate you deciding to get this one. I have done my best to make sure it is jampacked with helpful information. I hope you enjoy it.

Chapter 1: Changing Your Mindset

Money, or finances, may seem like a simple thing. We use it in our everyday lives to buy what we need, pay our bills, provide for our families, keep a roof over our heads, and do things that we want to in life. Money, in some form, is needed in just about every transaction across the planet. The progression throughout history is quite fascinating. At first, credit cards were a major deal. Now, there are countless digital ways to make financial transactions instantly with people all over the world. This evolution will continue, and it will be interesting to see where it goes.

The point here is that finance is such a major part of our lives. We need it in almost every single way. However, we actually know extraordinarily little about it. This is because we are taught to play it safe. It is as simple as that. The traditional mindset regarding finances is to avoid risky behavior as much as possible. From the time we are little kids, we are taught about money and the value that it brings in our lives. Many children had their own little piggy bank or jar where they kept their extra change. As they grew older, their parents may have opened a small bank account for them.

Eventually, children became teenagers and started earning more money through chores, jobs, or other avenues. Some even had the entrepreneurial spirit and opened up a lemonade stand, mowed the lawns in their neighborhood, or shoveled peoples' driveways during the winter. As they earned this money, they were learning the value of a dollar. For generations, parents have told their children that money is not easy to come by and must be treasured at every moment.

This has been the reality for many people around the world. The traditional mindset of earning money actively through work or business and then putting it in a savings account until you have enough money to retire someday is still a popular teaching point among the youth in this world. On the surface, there is really nothing wrong with doing any of this. It certainly is not illegal or unethical. When we earn our own money, we certainly value it more. We should value it more. Teenagers who simply borrow money from their parents may not understand the difficulty behind getting it. Once they start earning it themselves and stop relying on a financial backup, they suddenly take it much more seriously.

The great thing about the traditional mindset is that it keeps you safe. You earn whatever money you can and then stow it away in some type of checking or savings accounts. These accounts are insured, and your money grows a small percentage based on whatever the interest rate is. This is quite simple to do and requires little to no risk. That is until you no longer have the money coming in. In this manner, you begin losing exponentially. Money earned from a job or business income is great when it is there. When it goes away, so does that feeling of being safe.
I am not trying to turn this into a life advice book. I do want to point out, though, that playing it safe puts an immense amount of limitations on you. This holds

true whether talking about finances, or any other aspect of life. When we play it safe, we lose out on many things, and we ultimately take the biggest risk when we do not take any at all. This is because so many opportunities pass us by as we are terrified of pursuing them. We are afraid of going outside the box that was created for us.

Before we begin discussing the main topic at hand, our goal for this chapter will be to help you look at this from a different perspective. Basically, we want to challenge your mindset about money overall and change your financial mentality. We want to open up your mind to the potential of making more money by no longer thinking about it from the traditional sense. We want you to start thinking about investing.

Before we can go there, you must dismiss the idea of playing it safe. Investing requires a certain level of risk. With extra risk, comes extra chances for rewards. The bigger the risk, the bigger the reward. But then this also means the bigger the risk, the more chances you have to lose. When we begin thinking differently and come out of our secure bubble, we have to realize all of this. We must understand that thinking in an old-fashioned way is just that: old-fashioned. Taking risks creates extra opportunities we may not have even known existed. When we take them and win, we win a big way.

Of course, we realize that simply saying you need to change your mindset is not enough. Our beliefs, thoughts, and actions are often ingrained in us from childhood. They may even go back generations. Even as we become adults, the lessons, even lectures we received from our parents, remain in the back of our minds. Public schools do not offer many financial education courses unless they are electives. Even then, these classes offer curriculums that further teach the safe approach to handling money.

Most people remain living cushy lives and simply keep earning money from a job to put away for later. After decades of earning and saving, they may have enough to retire off of. Some people will suffer a major financial hardship, and there are a few approaches that can be taken from here. They can completely fall apart. They can work a second or third job to recover. They can seek out the help of family and friends or unemployment benefits until they are back on their feet. Or, they can completely change the course they have taken in life and start thinking about money in a whole new way. This is the direction we want to discuss here.

Increasing our financial mindset and acuity will take several steps. Since we have certain teachings indoctrinated into us, it will be difficult to just let them fall by the wayside. We have to work to change the way we think, but it will be worth it in the end. We will show you how. Before we specifically talk about shifting our financial mentality, we will discuss various other mindset alterations that must be adopted.

Please take note that we are not asking you to be careless with money, or not value it. You certainly should value the money you make because it was hard-earned. Calculated investing is not the same as gambling or throwing your money away. It is attempting to grow your wealth with a modicum of risk.

Learning to Take Risks

When we mention risks here, we are referring to reasonable and intelligent risk. Throwing your money at a fad because it promises to give you huge returns is not taking a risk; it is being irresponsible. An intelligent risk would be something that you have researched to the best of your ability, assessed the positive and negative aspects of, and then took a leap of faith on. Skydiving is risky, but getting the proper training, having the proper equipment, and listening to the instructions of the experts makes it somewhat reasonable. Skydiving without the proper training and preparation is just foolish, just like any other risk.

Risk-taking is simply defined as the act of sacrificing something personal to you, whether it be emotions, energy, time, money, or safety, to help improve your circumstances. In the case of skydiving, it was giving yourself a thrill that you may never have had before. Taking a risk means going beyond your comfort zone by exposing yourself to uncertainty. This sounds kind of scary. Do you want to backtrack and quit right now? I certainly hope not. When you are used to security, risk can be overwhelming. However, we can help you become more of a risk-taker by taking a few steps in the right direction.

Identify What You Want to Achieve:

You must fully understand what you want to achieve because it will clarify why you need to take a certain risk. Once you are clear about this, then it's time to recognize the potential outcomes and what results or consequences can come from those outcomes. Don't just look at what you can gain, but also at what you can lose. This is the only way to look at it objectively. If based on assessment, what you lose will be worth it based on what you could gain, then the risk should be worth it.

The next thing you must consider is the obstacles in your way. What can potentially keep you from obtaining your achievement, and how can you overcome it? When you think hard enough, there is usually always a solution. Once you understand the obstacles, then assess any other certainties you may have. What are some potential self-limitations you have? What is the worst thing that can happen? Ask yourselves these kinds of questions when assessing your ability to take a risk.

Assess Past Lessons:

Before undertaking any risky behavior, consider the lessons you have learned in the past. Do these lessons give you any insights into what is happening now? Anything that you have learned from experience may be utilized in the present time. Both successes and failures in your personal history can help you make more informed decisions right now. In addition, you can learn from other peoples' history. Either by witnessing it yourself or receiving advice.

If you have never done anything remotely similar to what you are about to undertake, then try to find the most relevant experiences you can to the current situation. Just because you have never experienced something, does not mean other lessons in your life cannot be relatable. Once you start searching honestly, you will not believe what you can learn from your past.

Develop a Plan of Action:

Outline a specific plan for how you want to proceed and a reasonable time frame that you are looking at. When you do this, also pinpoint the resources that you have or can somehow get. If there is specific training required, find out before you proceed. For example, if your goal is to become a firefighter in six months but have not even started the schooling or have the finances at your disposal, this is not a reasonable goal. You can still become a firefighter, but it won't happen in six months.

Also, consider the timing of the risk. Is it reasonable for you to take something based on your current schedule or situation? We want you to challenge yourself, but taking on way more than you can handle is not a responsible approach. Assess the potential negative consequences of your plan of action and ask yourself if you are equipped to handle them. Layout as detailed of a plan as you can and then get ready to move forward with some faith.

Decide Whether the Risk Is Worth Taking:

Based on the analysis you have done up to this point, decide if you are ready to jump in and take the risk. Is a particular risk worth taking? This is the time you start taking action without hesitation. If you are only halfway dedicated, your chance of success is much lower. We have already done our preplanning and preparation, and now it's time for fate to take over. You don't have to move fast. You just have to move forward.

Taking sensible risks generally involves having a purpose behind it. Meaning, there are motivating factors involved in taking a risk. In regard to the topic we are discussing here, the main motivator for taking money risks is to have more financial abundance. Once we have determined why and how we will proceed, it is time to focus our attention on our financial acuity.

Shifting the Money Mindset

Here is the bottom line. The traditional mindset about money has been limiting your financial mentality in a big way. It has hindered you and even prevents you from achieving the money success that you have the potential for. Essentially, it has been keeping you broke. We have heard countless times that mindset is what keeps people in poverty. This is a controversial statement, and many people do not understand what it means. We are not saying that you wake up every morning and are glad you don't have enough money to pay bills, fix repairs, feed your children, buy a nicer home, or travel to wherever your want. What we mean is that the way you think creates limitations on what you can do.

Instead of coming home and reading books, articles, or blogs about wealth, you simply plop on the couch and search for what is on television. Instead of saving up extra money to put into a high-yielding account or fund, you would much rather buy the latest trend or stop at your favorite coffee place for a five-dollar latte. Imagine how much money you could save monthly if you just cut the number of lattes you drink at a coffee shop by half. Let's say that you drink 30 lattes a month at five dollars apiece. Cutting out down to 15 would save you $75 in a month. That's $900 in a year, which is a fairly good chunk of change.

We realize we are making many generalizations here and apologize for that. You may not be spending money frivolously and are actually quite responsible. You may have some very legitimate reasons for struggling financially. We are simply here to help you start thinking about ways to change your money habits. Most of us have money management woes, and they can become quite detrimental if we do not address them properly.

While it may be a struggle, changing your money mindset is definitely possible. We can literally retrain our minds to think differently and start breaking the chains that have been put on us for so long. As adults, if we are open-minded, we can learn new things all of the time. We take adult education courses on learning new languages, painting, pottery, or even practicing a trade. We can certainly take the time to learn more about finances too.

For some reason, there is a resistance to all of this. It can certainly be due to the fact that money holds so much power in this world. There are so many things we cannot do without it. If we don't have it, we could lose everything, including our house, cars, friends, and family. Money is not something we feel comfortable losing. Honestly, you never really will feel this way. It is never fun to lose money, and whenever you do, it will hurt to a certain degree. The aim here is to get comfortable being uncomfortable. We discussed earlier the proper mindset of taking risks. Once we are better prepared for stepping out of our comfort zone, we are one step closer to a new money mindset.

Many individuals live with a scarcity mindset. This can be seen by how they handle money. People are either terrified of spending money, or they spend everything they earn the moment their check arrives. With the scarcity mindset, you will always be focused on not having enough money. Before you are able to invest with a certain level of comfort, you must learn to shift your thought-processes from scarcity to abundance.

Contrary to scarcity, the abundance mindset allows you to see things in a favorable light. You will become open to many different financial outcomes that are in your future. Instead of focusing on the limitations of your money matters, you will start seeing the hidden potential. When this happens, you will be prepared to create more wealth, because you will believe it is a possibility. If you open a business, for example, you will be able to imagine the customers lining up to buy your products or services. This does not mean you live in a fantasy world. Nor does it mean you are not prepared for potential problems to occur. They just are not the focal point of your mindset.

Financial expert and best-selling author, Robert Kiyosaki, discusses how people completely shut their minds off to making money. When people see something they cannot afford, they simply say, "I can't afford that," and then move on. This type of thinking shuts down their mind, and people immediately quit on themselves. You are being highly unfair to yourself by doing this. What people should be doing is asking the question, "How can I afford this?' This type of thinking keeps the mind open to many possibilities that exist in the world.

The abundance mindset goes hand in hand with the law of attraction theory. Essentially, when you focus on having more than enough money, you will attract it into your life. You will always have more than you need to meet your goals. The fear of never having enough will go away. There are ways you can alter your thinking to start believing in this manner. We will discuss some of these methods here.

Money Needs Direction:

You need to have a plan for what you will do with your money. You can have all of the money coming in; however, if you have no idea what to do with it or how to manage it, you will eventually lose it all. This is why so many people who have made millions of dollars end up completely broke. They did not have any type of plan for their money, or they executed it very poorly. You need to be different. You need to set up a financial plan immediately.

Cut Emotional Spending:

People often spend money based on their emotions and what is happening in their lives at the time. This can range from minor expenses like impulse buying at the store, or major expenses like buying a house that is way out of their price range. When people are extremely happy, they will celebrate by spending money. When life is not going great, they will use the money to try and feel better. Money creates a sense of power, so people will spend it to make themselves feel in control again.

You must understand that life will not always go as planned. There will be many ups and downs; however, this cannot cause you to become irresponsible with your money. You need to control your emotions to avoid rash decisions. In the investment world, this could mean selling a stock or buying rental property at an improper time.

Money Situations Are Personal

We are trying to keep up with the Jones. This is a phrase you have probably heard over and over again. Basically, this means we compare our lives to other people, and when we see ourselves falling short, as we inevitably do at some point, we feel like failures. This goes for money matters too. Very often, we compare our financial situations to those of our friends, family, neighbors, or coworkers. We feel like we must keep up or surpass them. Looking at your financial situation in this manner can create feelings of inferiority, envy, and despair.

Understand now that your finances are personal to you and not relative to someone else. This means that your success with money is based on reaching your own goals and not keeping up with someone else. You may see someone you know driving a fancy car, buying a new house, taking extravagant vacations, or always having the latest gadgets. These individuals may have an abundance of wealth they are able to spend, or they are just scraping by and only look wealthy. For all you know, they could be thousands of dollars in debt. Whatever the case, it should not be any of your concern. Other peoples' finances are not your business, so just focus on your own situation. Thinking in this manner will help you avoid spending irresponsibly just to keep up with those around you.

Change Your Money Script:

How do you find yourself talking about money and wealth? For example, when you see something out of your price range, do you say something like, "That is way too expensive, and I will never be able to afford it"? Do you tell yourself that you will never be as successful as you want? If so, then you have a negative money script. This creates severe financial blocks in our lives because we are putting limitations on ourselves. The way you think about money will affect your financial situation because our thoughts are what create action. Action is what creates results.

It is important to identify any negative money scripts in your life and change them to positive scripts. This is a great way to start shifting your scarcity mindset to that of abundance. Instead of saying, "I can never afford that," say, "I will figure out a way to afford that." Changing simple statements like this may not seem like a big deal; however, it will slowly shift your way of thinking and begin opening up your mind to the possibilities that may exist out there. This is a very simple tactic, but the results are tremendous.

As you try to change your finances, consider how the way you speak about yourself is holding you back. Determine if negative speech is sabotaging you. If you don't believe in yourself, you can never have an abundance mindset.

Money Is Not Evil

You may have heard the expression, "Money is the root of all evil." The actual has been altered throughout time; however, this particular statement suggests that all bad deeds, or evilness, in the world, stem from money and peoples' obsession with it. Money has truly received a bad image over the years as people have become obsesses with it and used it to perform some very cruel acts. Here is some hard truth, though. Money is not evil. In the end, the actions people take are evil.

Money is good when it's paying your bills, buying your food, keeping a roof over your head, or helping out a good cause. What is different here? What is being done with the money? Stop having a negative view of money and begin looking at it in a positive light. Imagine all of the great things you can do in this world when you have an abundance.

Take the phrase, "Money is the root of all evil," out of your mind, and stop blaming it for the bad things in this world. Once you shift your thought-process in this manner, you will begin attracting money into your life. After you have taken these steps to change your financial mentality, you are now ready to look at investing.

The Law of Attraction

We have touched on this concept throughout this chapter. We want to delve deeper into the law of attraction, especially as it relates to money. People misinterpret what the law of attraction really means. Honestly, you can't blame them either because of the many ways it has been presented. You cannot just sit in a yoga position all day and attract everything you want by just thinking about it. What this law really means is that what you think on the inside, the universe will manifest for you.

As it relates to money, how you feel and think about money is what the universe will ultimately create for you. If you are constantly shutting off your mind to making more money, then the universe will pick up on this, and your money woes will never go away. You will never be able to obtain wealth because the universe will not present you with the opportunities to do so. Here's another interesting fact. If you think about the concept of poverty from the negative point of view, you are still creating negative energy towards wealth. For example, if you are always thinking, "I hate being poor," the vibes you put out there are still of being poor and impoverished.

According to the law of attraction, you must always think of money in a positive sense. Instead of saying, "I hate being poor," say something like, "I want to become rich." Literally, change your vocabulary and take the idea of being poor completely out of your head. Once you have developed the mindset, it is time to get to work. You cannot simply think your way to wealth. Positive thinking opens up your mind and brings opportunities to light. You must have the fortitude to grab these opportunities and then work your tail off to make great things happen from them.

This is where the disconnect comes from. Thinking positively and working hard is what the law of attraction is all about.

Investing Basics

Investing can be divided into many sections and subsections. The basic definition, as it relates to finances, is to expend money in the expectation that you will receive some type of profit from it. This can also be called a return on investment. A simple example can be buying a home for a certain price, and then selling it a few years down the line for a higher price. The difference in the price you sold the home for versus the price you bought it for is the profit. The term investment has been used in relation to other aspects of our lives as well. For example, doing something positive towards your health is called investing in your health. For this book, we will be focusing on financial investments.

Investing takes a lot of time, fortitude, energy, patients, knowledge, and faith. I say faith because once you have done your research and taken appropriate action, then luck will play a major part in the results. Of course, luck cannot be the deciding factor. Especially for long term investing. At some point, skill needs to play a role too.

Investing can be complicated, especially when you are first starting out. There are many phrases, techniques, and paths to consider due to the high number of possibilities that exist. Investing never becomes easy, no matter how experienced you become. There will always be variables beyond your control, and there is no way to predict everything. The best route is to do your research well and have the qualities we mentioned above.

All of the mindset alteration techniques that we have discussed lead us up to this point. Without this change, we would never have the courage to invest. We would simply play it safe for the rest of our lives and avoid as much trouble as we can. It is true that the less risk you take, the less likely you are to have massive failures. However, you will live your life with limits and lose out on all sorts of money that is available to you out there.

As you invest more and more, you will lose more money. This is hard to avoid. You will not always be right, and you need to become okay with that. You need to be okay with falling flat on your face. Some of the greatest investors in history have lost more money than most people can even imagine having. This happened because they were willing to lay it on the line in order to gain large returns.

Warren Buffett, who is the grandmaster of investing in the stock market and a billionaire many times over, is consistently ranked as one of the richest men in the world. His net worth fluctuates big time, and it will be hard to predict what it will be by the time you read this section. Whatever the case, the rankings will show you what they are worth, but not how much they have lost along the way. Warren Buffett has lost billions over the decades. He is still considered one of, if not the most, successful investors of all time.

Our goal with this book is not to turn you into the next Warren Buffett. It this happens for you, then congratulations. We simply wanted to illustrate the mindset it takes to become an investor. You cannot be afraid to lose. You cannot dwell on being a failure, but on becoming as successful as you can. You must keep a positively focused mind through good and bad times.

When you are ready to invest, you have officially opened up your mind to all of the money that is out there. There truly is a large pot available, and once you understand how to access it, you will have the potential to create great wealth. Good investors are knowledgeable about ways that the market works.

Now that you are ready, we will help you understand this as well.

Chapter 2: Understanding the Other Side

Before we move onto the topic of passive funds, there are a few discussion points that must be gone over. You must understand these concepts because they will be your opponents during the investment process and even obstacles you must overcome. If you don't understand these concepts and become prepared for them, they will destroy your investment portfolio. We will discuss these points one-by-one.

Inflation

In the world of economics, this is the measure of the rate at which the average price level of specific goods and services increases over a time period. Basically, after a certain amount of time, a set currency amount will be less valuable in the marketplace. For example, $20 in the year 1990 would buy you a certain amount of apples. However, due to inflation over time, the value of apples goes up, so $20 will buy you fewer apples.

In a jocular fashion, this concept is often made light of when an older generation states that a certain amount of money was like having riches back in the day. "When I was a kid, 50 cents was a lot of money." How many times have we heard this phrase before? As you've grown older, many necessary items have raised in price, whether it was gas, food, cars, land, real estate, or entertainment. A rise in inflation indicated a reduced purchasing power of a national currency.

As the currency loses its value with inflation, the overall cost of living for the general public rises significantly. The loss of purchasing power all of this creates leads to a major slow down in economic growth. Most economists agree that inflation occurs when the money supply of a particular nation hurdles economic growth. A countries main monetary authority does what is necessary to make sure inflation does not get out of control and to keep the economy running smoothly. The monetary authority is something like a central bank. There are certain measures these organizations can take to keep everything within acceptable limits.

There are numerous causes of inflation. Rising prices are at the root of this issue. Inflation cause can be classified into three different categories.

- Demand-pull effect: This type of inflation occurs when the demand for particular goods and services heavily outweighs the economy's capacity to produce them. This high demand, low supply situation leads results in higher prices of said product or service. For example, if a particular car manufacturer reduces the number of cars it makes, the supply diminishes. If the demand stays the same or increases, this will create a supply-demand gap, so the manufacturer will raise prices due to the public wanting the car, and this will lead to inflation.

- Cost-push effect: This is the result of increased prices during the production process. For example, labor costs may go up, or the price of raw materials may increase, resulting in higher costs of the end product or service. For example, housing prices may skyrocket due to increased costs of wood, glass, cement, and other raw materials.
- Built-in inflation: As the price of goods and services rises, laborers expect and demand higher wages. This is to maintain the cost of living to keep up with rising prices. These increased wages result in further increases in the cost of goods and services, and the cycle continues from here.

Inflation will never go away, except for a few instances. The overall price of goods and services will not be what they were 50 years ago, and prices 50 years from now will be much higher than today. There are numerous monetary policy measures that can be implemented to help control inflation. However, these are grossly out of the control of the average person and is generally falls on the shoulders of financial regulars, like the central bank.

Inflation can be beneficial or detrimental, depending on the vantage point of the individual. People who are holding stocks or investment properties may enjoy inflation as they will see an increase in the value of their assets. People looking to buy investments or hold onto cash may not be fond of inflation because they will have to spend more money. The key here is to maintain an optimal level of inflation and not let it get out of control. This way, buyers will feel comfortable spending, and investors will continue to see a rise in their portfolios.

While inflation may be beyond your control, that does not mean that you cannot manage it in certain ways. You can take certain actions to help preserve your savings and investments, so you don't lose all of your money. Diversifying your portfolio can be one way of shielding your money against inflation. However, diversifying does not guarantee protection against the loss of funds, nor will it guarantee returns.

Inflation-protected Securities, or IPS, investments have a rate of return that is adjusted for inflation, so there is a guarantee of a return in the end. Examples of IPS investments include Treasury Inflation-Protected Securities from the federal government or Corporate Inflation-Protected Securities that come from private sector companies.

Stocks can also hedge your investments against inflation. The rise in stock prices usually goes hand-in-hand with inflation. If you are currently holding onto a stock and inflation occurs, your particular holdings have increased in value.

We could write books all day about what inflation is and how it can affect different people. The main purpose of this section is to help you understand that inflation must not be ignored if you are entering the investment world. The more you understand it, the more you can use it to your advantage. If you don't monitor inflation and what it can create, you will end up on the losing end almost every time.

Big Banks

Big banks do not have the greatest reputation these days. There have been many incidents in the recent past that have created a large distrust with the general public. Much of this distrust is justified, while some of it may be based on falsities. Whatever the case, we are not here to discuss that right now. Banking institutions can be a great avenue for investing based on several important factors.

- Banks provide a societal function that is very necessary and will never go away.
- A business model of a bank is relatively easy to understand. They take in money from people who create various types of accounts and use this capital for various types of interest rate loans like mortgages.
- Many banks stocks trade at a bargain rate so an investor can get in with limited capital. You do not have to take out a loan or second mortgage to invest.

Bank stocks can be a great addition to your investment portfolio. There are three different types of banks listed below:

- Commercial banks: This is the typical type of bank you would see where you go to make deposits and various other transactions.

- Investment banks: Investment banks are generally hired by organizations to assist with complex financial transactions. This type of banking involves raising capital for individuals, corporations, and governments, and giving advice on mergers, acquisitions, and corporate restructuring. Investment banks do not take deposits like retail and commercial banks.
- Universal banks: These types of banks provide services of both commercial and investment banks. Universal banks are much more common in Europe. They have been slow to grow in the United States due to strict regulations.

While bank stocks can be beneficial, they are not a full-proof investment strategy. There are a few things to consider when analyzing bank stocks. It's important that the banks have quality loans. Poor lending practices of the past is what led to many financial crisis situations of the past. The following are some bank risk metrics to look at.

- Non-performing loan (NPL) ratio: These are loans that are close to default, and at least 90 days overdue. Having a high percentage of these loans is not a sign of a healthy portfolio. To calculate this ratio, take the amount of money in non-performing loans and divide it by the total number of outstanding loans. Then, take this number and multiply it by 100. For example, if an institution has 7 billion in NPL and 950 billion total in overall loans,

that's a 0.7% ratio. Anything higher than two percent should be a cause for concern. A high NPL means that banks are giving out too many loans to unqualifying individuals who are then defaulting on them. While much of this is on the borrower, it also shows extreme irresponsibility from the lender.
- Coverage of bad loans: as we mentioned before, loans given are not always paid back. Un repaid loans are tracked and called loan loss provisions or coverage of bad loans. The coverage of bad loans equals the allowance of loan loss provisions divided by the total non-preforming loans. The final number will be a percentage after multiplying by 100. For example, if a banking institution set aside 10 billion dollars for loan loss provisions, and had an NPL of 6.5 billion, then they have 153% for bad loan coverage. As long as the institution has more money set aside for bad load coverage than the actual amount of bad loans, then this is a good sign.
- Net charge-offs: This is a statement from the lending bank that the loan amount given will probably not be repaid. They usually declare this statement after about six months of delinquency without any payments. To get the NCO, you take the NCO's divided total loans and then multiplied by 100. For example, if the net charge-off is 4 billion, and 900 billion in total loans, then the net charge-off rate is 0.44%. The best way to assess this number is to compare it to the industry average at the time.

During poor economic cycles, fewer loans get paid off.

Big banks can be a major opponent for you as you start investing. If you learn how they work, you can create large advantages from them. Many people see banks as the enemy. This does not have to be the case with you.

Promoters

When you hear the word promoter, you are probably thinking of someone who promotes or brings attention to certain sporting or entertainment events. Promoters also exist within the investment world and work in a similar fashion. Their goal is to raise money for particular investment activity. These promoters seek out potential investors and bring information about specific investments to their attention. Their ultimate aim is to seek out capital to bring towards the investment opportunity they are promoting before it lands somewhere else. The more capital they bring in, the more advantages they receive.

There are several different types of promoters you should be aware of.

- Penny stock promoter: These are individuals or entities that promote the penny stock market, which are small companies with lower-priced shares. These promoters can be those who give positive testimonials to bring in more excitement around a particular investment.

>   This will cause shares of the small company to increase and bring in more revenue.
- Government-based trade promoter: This is when government entities assist US companies with promotion to foreign markets.
- Casual promoters: These are the customers or clients that work with a particular business and have a good experience. They will then share this good experience with the public, which can bring in more customers and potential investors.

An honest promoter is someone you can trust and will bring you solid information in good faith. Issues arise when dishonest promoters give false impressions of an investment opportunity. They may purposely withhold information to make the opportunity seem full proof. Many promoter have been linked to illegal activity due to major scams.

As an investor, you must learn to do your own research and not allow promoters to completely persuade you one way or the other. These individuals also have a financial interest based on how much capital they can bring in. Realize that they may have their own interests at heart and not yours. It is certainly okay to listen to them, but don't take their words as gospel. The biggest advantage a promoter can have for you is to bring attention to a certain opportunity you may not have otherwise known about. From here, you can do your own research.

Your Biggest Opponent

We will not discuss your biggest opponent when it comes to investing and life in general. The opponent is you. No other individual will get in your way for investment success more than yourself. We spoke earlier about mindset. If you do not develop the proper mindset for investing, you will likely never start, let alone succeed. As you invest, realize that certain things will not work out in your favor. Even if you do all of the research and perform as you are supposed to, things can still go wrongs. Do not allow this to stop you. Learn from your mistakes and have the fortitude to keep moving forwards.

There are many investment errors people make as they go along. While there is no way to prevent all mistakes, understanding some of the most common ones can keep you from becoming your own worst enemy. The following are a few things you should avoid when entering into the realm of investing.

- Not understanding the company or investment. Many people invest in businesses simply because they've heard about their success but have done no actual research on them. They are essentially going in blindly, hoping for the best. Warren Buffett, the world's most successful investor, warns against investing in companies where you do not understand the business model.
- Avoid falling in love with a company because it can skew your focus. When a company makes you money, it's easy to forget why you bought into it in the first place. You fall so much in

love with the company that you become blind to many of the faults that come up. You may not recognize the company breaking down right in front of your eyes because you choose to ignore it. Always keep in mind that it's for business and profit. Once a company is not bringing you profit, consider selling.
- Patience is a virtue, and a lack of it is detrimental. With any type of long-term success in life, you will have to make slow and steady progress. This includes investing. You must take a very disciplined approach because there will be many ups and downs. You must keep your focus and understand that impulsive decisions will bring a downfall in regard to future financial success.
- Attempting to time the market is exceedingly difficult, even for experienced investors. Do not even consider it if you are a novice.
- Fast turnover during investment or collecting cash too often can be detrimental financially as transaction fees, and short-term tax rates will eat up profits. If you are lucky, you will break even after all of the fees or just barely make a profit. Furthermore, you can miss out on some long-term future gains. This idea goes along with the timing of the market and having patience.
- Waiting to break even is a mistake investors make. This means that you are holding on to a losing investment in the hopes of it increasing in value again so you can at least sell it for what it's worth. While this may occur, the chances

are, you will be losing in two fashions. In the first place, the investment could go down further and become worthless. Second, you could be missing out on potential winners by not pulling out your capital and using it somewhere else.
- Diversifying your portfolio is to shield you from losing excess money and having gains overall. Many people do not do this and rely on one or two things to take them into financial freedom. For example, certain investments in your portfolio may not be doing well, while others will be thriving. Unless you are a high-level investor, stick to the principle of diversification.
- People let their emotions rule them. I will let you know now that investing of any kind will give you unbelievable highs and tragic lows if you do it long enough. This will create a varying amount of emotions within you. Do not let these emotions rule you. For example, do not get into any investment without doing your research because the opportunity excites you, and don't sell an investment without thinking it through because you are scared. Keep your emotions under control.

In the end, you will become your biggest opponent. While investing will always come with a level of uncertainty, you must do your research and proceed in a manner that is best for you. Challenge yourself to constantly become a better investor.

I want you to become familiar with the opponents you will be dealing with as you begin your investing lifestyle. There will be more that come up beyond these four. I don't want these obstacles to deter you from becoming a successful investor. Again, I am not trying to turn you into Warren Buffett here. If this book is your starting point and you end up being the next great worldwide investor, then that is terrific. Realize, though, that you will need to push through and redirect yourself many times along the way. The more you invest, the more challenges you will face. Acknowledge them, learn about them, respect them, but don't be controlled by them.

Chapter 3: Passive Investment Funds

Considering what we have covered already about investing, there are numerous avenues you can take. Many investors can perform and make millions of dollars in their sleep. These people know what they are doing and how to utilize the market to their advantage. They are well-experienced and have been around the block many times. Of course, there are numerous experienced investors who still struggle to make big money. Many novice investors start off slow and then work their way up. Some individuals remain conservative for their entire lives. In this book, we will go by the assumption that you are a new investor. For this reason, we will provide for you a safe approach in entering the market to make extra money through passive investment funds.

Passive investing is a strategy used to maximize returns by minimizing buying and selling. In a broad sense, it refers to a buy-and-hold strategy for long-term horizons. The methods used in this type of investing strategy aim to avoid fees and limited performance times that occur with frequent trading that come with active investment strategies. The main assumption when following passive investment strategies is that the market will post positive returns over time. They do not rely on short-term fluctuations. Passive investment funds are a safe approach to entering the investment world.

Active Investing

Before we delve further into passive investing strategies, we will describe what active funds are. As you become a more comfortable investor, this may be an approach you can take in the future. Active funds require a more human element to them, such as fund managers, who can monitor these investments closely and make real-time decisions. Individuals and companies who follow the active strategy believe they can time the market and even outperform it.

Active management seeks to produce higher and quicker returns than passive funds. The methods required are difficult to master, and as we mentioned before, even the most experienced investors have a hard time doing it. Some of the advantages of active management include:

- Having a manager who is an expert in a particular industry, like automotive.
- There is flexibility in the investments you can purchase, and the ability to buy and sell as needed is quite accessible. Timing the market is a big part of this.
- The potential to make greater amounts of money over a short period of time is there.
- There are numerous takes advantages that come with these types of funds.

Overall, active fund management is a much more aggressive type of investing that some with a potential for greater returns but poses higher risks. The results here depend on the skills of the individual investor or manager.

Passive Funds Pros and Cons

Now that we understand what active management funds are, our focus for this book will be passive investment funds. Maintaining a diversified portfolio is an important investment strategy and the foundation for passive funds. Index funds are a form of passive investing that creates diversity by spreading out the risk. They do this by holding a large number of securities in their benchmark. These types of funds target a benchmark, or index, and do not seek out winning investments. In this manner, they avoid constantly buying and selling securities. This means that they have lower fees and expenses than actively managed funds. While active funds must be monitored actively by a manager, passive investments like index funds track an index, so they are an easy way to invest in a chosen market.

Besides the ultra-low fees and reduced risks of passive fund investments, there are numerous other benefits. First of all, there is a lot of transparency, as you will always know which assets are involved. The buy-and-hold strategy does not usually result in massive capital gains taxes over the year. Finally, owning an index fund or other group of indices is much easier and less work than an active fund. With an active fund, there is a lot of strategy involved, which requires constant research and adjustment. If you don't pay attention to an active fund for a while, you could take a serious hit. This will not likely occur with a passive fund because active involvement is not needed.

Just like with anything good, passive funds do have their downfalls. You should at least be aware of these so you are fully informed. Generally, proponents of active funds have the following critiques of passive funds.

- They are way too limited. Passive funds follow a predetermined set of investments with very little deviation allowed. This means investors are locked into holdings despite what the market may be doing. Lack of flexibility turns off active investors in a big way. They are essentially stuck with stocks, even if they are performing poorly. Other stocks in their index can offset these losses if they are doing well.
- They have smaller potential returns. Passive funds, by their definition, will never beat the market. Their holdings are locked in to track the market, even during times of great turmoil. The only time a major return will occur is when the market booms in a major way. Still, it will pale in comparison to active funds.

Index funds are considered ideal for various retirement accounts like 401ks or IRAs. Legendary investor Warren Buffett calls them a haven for savings to use for the later years in life. Most people are not full-time investors. They have regular careers, families, hobbies, and other interests that take up the majority of their time. They may not have the ability to invest aggressively. In this sense, index funds and other passive investment strategies make more sense. It allows the average person to buy stocks in various companies at a low cost and then have decent returns over a long period of time.

If you open up a retirement account at a young age and deposit a certain amount of your savings on a regular basis, you have the potential to make hundreds of thousands or even millions by the time you reach retirement age. Of course, this depends largely on how much you invest and how well the market does. If you buy stock in a particular company, you have a much better chance of seeing positive gains over a 40-year period, than a one- or two-year period. Once you open any type of passive fund investment account, set aside a certain amount of money from your income to deposit every month. Do not plan on taking it out until you retire, unless there is a major emergency that requires it.

The goal when diversifying an index fund is that the broad spectrum of holdings mimics a certain "index," which can be the whole stock market or a section of it. The fund will then match the performance of the index. An index fund exists for almost every financial market in the world. The United States has several indexes, and the most popular one is the S&P 500. Other major ones include the Dow Jones Industrial Average, Nasdaq Composite, Barclays, and Willshire 5,000 Total Market Index, among others. An index fund that follows the Dow Jones would invest in the same companies that comprise this particular index. The index may be weighted, meaning a higher percentage of the funds will be geared towards certain securities over others. A portfolio manager can help restructure and re-balance these percentages from time-to-time.

Index Fund Categories

One of the great things about index funds is that they do not all fit into a single category. There are different types of these funds that can fit into anyone's taste. The first index fund was created in 1976, and it has become more complex and varied since then. These varied types of index funds give access to additional markets, sectors, and investment styles.

Broad Market:

This type of index tries to capture a large section of the market to invest in. These investments include stocks, bonds, and any other type of security. Broad market indexes have very low expense ratios, and with the low turnover of securities, they provide a lot of tax efficiency. This fund will give you the most diverse basket of securities. If you decide to invest in the broad market, careful about holding other indexes. You may have some overlap in securities.

International:

International index funds can provide a lot of outside exposure for you. Many of the broad market indexes focus on US-based companies. With the international index, you can benefit from companies in Europe, Africa, Asia, Australia, and Oceania. The only place that's off the market is Antarctica. These types of funds are not always tied to particular regions like the Middle East or Central America.

Term-based Bonds:

These are good for fixed-term investors. Having a good mix of short, intermediate, and long-term bonds can provide a stable income for many years.

Municipal Bonds:

These bonds do not pay federal taxes, and often are also exempt from state and local. The latter is only true when the bond is issued in the same state investor lives. If you live in a state with high state and local taxes, consider only looking for these types of bonds in your specific area. This will shield you from major taxes being withheld from you.

Earnings-based:

There are two types of indexes involved in this section: growth and value indexes. Growth indexes are made up of companies that are expected to grow their earnings faster than the market overall. Value indexes are made up of stocks at a low price relative to the company's earnings. Growth stocks are much more volatile than value stocks, so they rise quickly when the market is going up and fall quickly when the market is down. Since value stocks' prices are already low, they do not fall much when the market is down. Also, they lag behind the overall market as it goes up.

Sectors:

You can choose to invest in specific sectors of the market, like real estate. The sectors can be broad like technology, or very specific, like cloud computing. Many investors want exposure to a particular industry, but don't know which one to choose. In this manner, they can invest in a sector fund and allow the market to figure out which company will be good to bet on.

As you can see, Index funds provide a wide array of options for you. While particular indexes will limit you once you get involved, you can still choose from a large variety before you jump in. You can also hold multiple indexes at the same time, just avoid overlap of specific securities when you do.

Dividend-Focused:

A dividend is a sum of money that is paid regularly, and generally on a quarterly basis. There are two types here: growth and yield. Dividend growth indexes include companies that consistently raise their dividends and have the potential to keep doing so in future practices. Dividend yield indexes are those with high dividend-yielding stocks. These index funds are great for investors seeking consistent income from their investments.

ETFs Versus Mutual Funds

Many individuals get exchange-traded funds (ETFs) and mutual funds mixed up because they do have a lot in common. They both provide a mix of funds from many different assets. They are a great way for people to diversify their portfolios. Both of these are good options for safer investments over trying to pick individual securities on your own.

Mutual funds are actually actively managed by a fund manager who makes critical decisions on how to allocate specific assets. Mutual funds can only be purchased at the end of a trading day. Overall, mutual funds do try to beat the market and create more short-term funds for the investor. They are still good long-term investment options due to their diversity. If you regularly invest in a mutual fund and it does well over time, you can have more than enough money to retire off of.

ETFs are more in line with what we are discussing here. They are passively managed funds that typically track a specific market index. As a result, EFTs have lower fees and are less risky than mutual funds. However, the potential for high profit is less likely. With EFT funds, the stocks can be traded throughout the day. The lower chance of capital gains also gives a major tax advantage over mutual funds. Finally, EFTs are easier to get into as they require less capital than a mutual fund. Typically, you can get in for as low as the price of one share.

Precious Metals

Precious metals are rare metals found naturally in the earth and have a high level of value. Societies around the world appreciate them more, and individuals are willing to hand over more cash then they would for base metal. Due to their properties, precious metals are more useful in terms of products that can be created from them, like jewelry and art.

Since these precious metals hold so much value, they are a great investment option for long-term, passive growth. The precious metals we are discussing here are palladium, platinum, gold, and silver. Some people hold these metals in physical forms, such as gold and silver bars, or various personal items that are made from them. You can choose to go this route and keep them locked up in a safe or lockbox for security. Another option is to have a precious metals' passive investment account. This means you can create something like an IRA dedicated to precious metals and allow it to grow passively over time. Just like other passive investment funds, these will be managed by an expert in the field, so there will be a certain amount of fees to cover these costs.

The great thing about precious metals is that they are highly valued on a global scale and not affected by the currency values of individual countries. Holding investments in things like gold and silver can help offset the losses incurred by other investments. For example, inflation will cause the value of the dollar to fall, but gold and other precious metals will continue to rise. This is a great way to hedge against your multitude of investments.

Precious metal investment accounts can be purchased through various brokerage firms dedicated to these options. Research which ones have the highest ratings and discuss the various options with an expert there.

Bear Market and Bull Market

As you invest, you will hear the terms bear market and bull market constantly. We want to clarify these terms for you. These terms are used to describe the market conditions, which will be a major force that determines your portfolio value. Bear and bull markets can also denote investors' attitudes because they are the ones who determine the market based on their actions.

A bear market is one that is actively on a decline. Typically, a 20% or greater fall denotes a bear market condition. Share prices continue on a downward trend, and investors believe they will continue to spiral lower. During this trend, the economy will slow down, and companies may start laying off employees. Think of a bear. When a bear is standing upright with its paws, it will come down to attack or pursue its prey. This is why the bear symbolizes a descending market.

A bull market, on the other hand, is when the market is ascending. The bull's horns are going up. During this time, prices are consistently rising, and investors believe the trend will continue to go up. During the bull market, the economy is up, and employment levels are high.

A bear versus bull market is typically determined by long-term activity. Short term swings, whether up or down, are more related to a particular event and do not signify a trend of any sort. Markets can also go through a series of upward and downward movements as they try to find direction. In these cases, we cannot always determine if it's a bear or bull market.

Both bear and bull markets have an effect and will influence your investments in a major way. During the bull market, you can buy more securities as they will increase in price. During the bear market, investors typically short-sell their assets as they are expecting great losses by staying in. Some investors will continue holding onto a security because they expect a gain in the future. However, they will likely lose money in a bear market before gaining once more. It can be risky to do this.

There are several factors to consider when determining the direction of a market. You can assess these in order to decide whether you are in a bear or bull market. Always remember that it can be difficult to figure out, even for seasoned investors.

- During a bull market, we see strong demand for securities, but a weak supply. There are many investors ready to buy up securities, but very few who are willing to sell. This signifies that investment values are on the rise, and people are not willing to give them up. Share prices will continue to rise because investors will be fighting over available equities or potential liquid assets. During a bear market, more individuals are looking to sell than buy.

- Share prices drop significantly because demand is lower than supply.
- Investor psychology and sentiment about the market conditions will also determine if there is a rise or fall. During a bull market, investors have high hopes and will be willing to participate in the hopes of making profits. During a bear market sentiment is low, and investors will begin moving money out of active funds and begin putting them into fixed-income securities. The decline in the stock market share prices will shake investors' confidence, and they will keep their money out until they start seeing some positive moves.
- The stock market and economy are strongly linked. When businesses are suffering, people are spending less, and stock prices will go down. When businesses are doing well, people spend more, which causes stock prices to go up.

Consider these various factors when trying to determine a bear versus bull market. To take advantage of both market trends, passive investment funds are a safe and reliable path to pursue. These will always provide less volatility during unpredictable markets, and the long-term success rate will be high.

Stocks, Bonds, and Liquid Assets

As you go through the investment process, you will come across some new lingo along the way. As you come across new words and phrases you do not recognize, it is important to look them up to help prevent any major confusion. A simple google term will usually work. If you are speaking to a financial advisor and they are using language you do not understand, ask them to clarify things. Any decent financial adviser will do so without hesitation. We will go over some common phrases you will here as you start investing in passive funds.

Stocks:

This is a form of investment that allows ownership share of a particular company. For example, if you have stocks invested in Coca Cola, you have partial ownership of this company. You are called a shareholder because you will share in the companies profits. You may also be able to make decisions about the companies future. Investors can buy stocks in order to grow their money. As the value of a particular share increases, people who invested in that stock share in these profits. If you bought ten shares of a stock for a price of $15 a share, your initial investment was $150. If the price goes up to $20 a share, your investment is now worth $200, giving you $50 in profits. Of course, share prices can go down, too, causing a shareholder to lose money. Stocks can be purchased individually through the stock exchange, or as part of a fund, like an index or ETF.

Bonds:

Bonds are often called fixed-income securities. When governments or private corporations need money for various projects, continue current operations, or refinance their debt, they will issue bonds to their investors. These bonds are essentially loans with interest payments that will be made. This means that when you purchase bonds, not only will you get back what you put in, but also the interest that's earned on these bonds. After a bond is purchased by an investor, they do not have to wait until the security date to sell. They can sell them at any point to make profits. Bonds are much safer than stocks because you won't lose money. This also means you don't have the same potential for returns. Most funds and portfolio models are a mixture of stocks and bonds. The higher risk portfolios have more stocks than bonds.

Liquid Assets:

This is a type of asset that can easily be converted into cash. For example, regular savings or checking accounts are considered liquid because you can immediately receive cash from them. Things like real estate, gold, silver, and various investment portfolios are not considered liquid assets because they cannot be quickly converted to cash for legal tender. Liquid assets are very important for businesses and individual investors because they are the first source of cash that is used for financial transactions and obligations.
There are many more financial terms that will come up as you go. It is definitely a language all to itself.

Hiring a Financial Planner

Unless you actually work in the financial industry, it can be difficult to make time for your own finances. In addition, it can get confusing when you gain access to different types of investments and strategies. Most people are not financial experts and don't have time to become one. This is why financial advisors exist. Financial advisors are experts in their field who help people tackle issues related to wealth management and personal finances. They can put together an entire savings plan and investment portfolio for you.

If you are looking for extra help and are overwhelmed by your finances, then finding a planner may be right for you. There are many great experts out there, so just do your research. Take a great amount of caution, though. Financial advising is largely an unregulated field. This means almost anyone can hang a sign on their door and call themselves a financial advisor. Look for individuals with industry credentials, like a certified financial planner license. Also, ask around and get reviews on particular people. Do not blindly follow someone because they are an expert. Remember, a financial planner will cost money too. Find the best person you can for your particular needs. Here are some questions to ask prior to hiring someone.

- Do you have experience working with clients like me?
- How much will you charge? Will you make money from the investments I choose?
- How often will we meet to discuss our financial plans?
- Are there any limitations on how often I can contact you?

Remember, with advanced technology and communication methods, there are several ways you can contact a financial planner. You don't even have to work with someone in your area. Just make sure they are readily accessible in other ways. Make sure that having a financial planner will be worth it and expect to have a long-term relationship. Many financial planners offer free consultations. Take advantage of these and even meet with several individuals before making a decision. It is your right because it is your money.

The aim of this chapter was to introduce you to one of the safest methods for entering into the financial world. Passive investment funds are a stable bet if you want more long-term growth of your money that a regular savings or checking account will not provide. The risk is certainly not zero; however, the chance of losing large amounts of money or going bankrupt is quite low, especially compared to more actively managed funds.

Chapter 4: Learning to Save

We will return back to the idea of saving in this chapter, which may seem counterintuitive to investing. However, part of investing is having enough capital to do so. There are many financial gurus out there touting the philosophy of "using other peoples' money" when investing. We are not giving our opinion one way or the other about this philosophy. We simply will not be discussing it here. In this chapter, we will detail the traditional methods of saving money so that you can have enough on hand to put into passive investment funds and other investment opportunities.

One of the purposes of this book is to do our best to make sure you do not go broke. This is why we have gone over safe and reliable investing methods. Saving properly is another simple philosophy; however, it is not easy for people to do. We will go over various ways to save money so you can feel financially secure in every way.

Creating A Budget

This is one of the most basic principles when it comes to saving money. We always hear about the word budget. The focus here is to categorize your income and expenses so that you are spending significantly less than what you make. This is certainly a fundamental concept, but once you enter the real world and begin dealing with real numbers, it can get quite complicated, especially when you start dealing with unexpected expenses.

The first technique you must get into the habit of is "PYF." Any basic financial or economic course will teach you this concept. It means to pay yourself first. When people receive their income, whether it is through a check or other course, they tend to pay themselves last. This means they will pay their bills and debts, buy groceries and other necessities, go out for entertainment, and get gifts for others before setting something aside for themselves. If they are lucky, they will have money left over to put away. You need to flip this around. Pay yourself first by setting aside a small percentage of your income in savings before spending money on anything else. Ten percent is a good number to shoot for.

Let's say you receive $1000 weekly. Before doing anything else, set aside $100 dollars and put it away into some type of savings account. You have already prevented yourself from spending everything you earn. Now, you can use the $900 dollars that are remaining and ration it appropriately between all of your expenses. Whatever you have leftover of the $900 should also be put away in your savings. If you can afford to pay yourself more than 10 percent, then definitely do so. Once you build up a steady saving's account, you can start moving the money over into an EFT or index fund.

In the end, it does not matter how much you make; it matters how much you keep. There are countless stories out there of millionaire athletes and actors spending all of their money and going broke. These individuals did not understand the basic concepts of managing money. Look at your own finances and determine right now how you can manage them. It may be easier than you think. Use the following steps to set up a solid budget plan.

- To start, calculate your expenses. It may be easier to calculate monthly expenses because most bills are due once a month. However, you can break it down further into weekly and daily expenses. You can also add up everything you spend over a six to 12-month period and then divide it down to get an average monthly expense tally. Be as thorough as you can, and make sure you do not miss any bills. Doing so can throw a major wrench into your budget plan. To give yourself extra room for unknown or unexpected expenses, you can add an extra 10 or 15 percent to your final expense number. For example, if you determine your total monthly expenses are $2000, add an additional $200 to it, to make the final number $2200.

- Now that we have calculated our expenses, it is time to add up our income. Your income is anything that you bring in on a monthly basis like your paycheck, investment incomes, alimony, child support, cash gifts or money from side gigs, etc. Once again, you can add up income over six to 12 months and then divide it down to get a monthly average. We also advise that you subtract 10 percent of your income from the total, so this money is stowed away from the beginning and not calculated into your budget. So, if your monthly income is $3,000, subtract $300 from it, making your total $2700 dollars. This will be the final number you will be working with on creating your budget.
- Subtract your expenses from your income to determine if you have a budget shortfall or overage. If we used the numbers from above, then we would be in an overage, which is good. You should always make more than what you spend. If you are in a shortfall, determine what expenses you can cut out or how you can raise your income. Are you buying a five-dollar cup of coffee every morning? That's $150 dollars a month. This expense may need to go or at least be reduced.
- Once you have a comfortable overage amount every month, then start setting savings and personal debt payoff goals. The savings are on

- top of the 10 percent you already put aside by paying yourself first.
- Stay on top of your finances by keeping a record of your spending and income. There are numerous online spreadsheets and budgeting apps you can use. You can also use the old-school method of pen and paper if that's what you prefer. Whatever the case, be diligent in keeping track of your money.
- Stick to your budget as much as possible. You break it once in a while, which is okay. Make sure this does not become a common practice get back on track as soon as possible.

When you create a solid budget and stick to it, you will see your savings account going up significantly. These savings can be used for investments later on so you can increase your income over the long haul. Start setting up your budget today.

Keeping Your Money Safe

You may have heard of several methods for keeping your money safe. Just like with investing, having your money spread out through various accounts is optimal. For example, you can set up a savings account strictly for money that you save and do not ever touch. You can also have various other accounts set up simultaneously for different reasons. A checking account can be used for making payments on personal items and bills, while another checking account can be set up for business expenses like work-related items, uniforms, or office supplies, etc. If you happen to own a business, it is advisable to set up a separate expense account solely for business expenses.

You can also keep a certain amount of cash at home to help you cover emergency expenses when a credit card or check option is not available. Below is a breakdown of how you can spread out your money to avoid putting it into a single account. Our total liquid amount will be $10,000.

- Regular saving's account: $2,000
- Emergency saving's account: $2,000
- Checking account: $3,000
- Business Account: $2,000
- Cash at home: $1,000

This is just an example, and you can certainly set up your own accounts; however, you please. As you gain more income, you can continue to spread it throughout these accounts as you see fit. We will now go over some specific bank accounts you can open up to help keep your money safe and secure. You can open a variety of these accounts and spread your funds throughout all of them. You can even have accounts in multiple banks if you feel that will help you. For many people, it is easier to save money if it's not in a single place, so consider diversifying your funds.

Regular Checking Accounts:

This is a very basic account at a bank where you can deposit money and take it out as you please by using checks, debit cards, or an ATM. There are various promotions and interest rates that may work to your advantage when opening up this basic account, so look into getting the best deal for yourself. This type of account is the most common one people use to pay their bills. Your best bet here may be to get a high-yield account so you can gain some extra interest while your money is sitting there.

Dividend Checking Accounts:

These specialized types of accounts are also called interest checking accounts as they offer higher interest rates. These are basically a combination of checking and savings accounts. They provide a higher interest rate as a savings account while letting you withdraw funds like a checking account without any penalties. With these types of accounts, you must maintain a minimum balance set by the institution. Be mindful that it does not drop below this level, or you will not be able to take advantage of the interest rates, plus you will incur some penalties. Interest rates depend on what is set by the federal government. You can assess these fees and determine when it is best to open this type of account.

Savings Account:

A regular savings account is one that encourages people to build up the wealth they earn. It often discourages withdrawals in the form of penalties. A savings account is a good place to store money to have for emergencies or to just sit there forever until you want to transfer it to someone else. Whatever the case, it is not to be looked at in the same manner as a checking account. They offer higher interest rates, so you are enticed to put more away in savings.

These types of accounts are not typically used for paying bills. Always use your checking account for these activities. You may be able to transfer money between accounts within an institution without a penalty. Sometimes, the transfers are unlimited, while other times, they can only be done a certain amount of times within a month. Discuss the terms with your banking institution. When opening up a savings account, look for the following criteria:

- Easy access to funds
- Online access
- Mobile friendly
- Federal deposit insured

Money Market Account:

These types of accounts will pay interest based on the current rates of the money markets in an individual country. If your nation's interest rates are high, then these accounts will be beneficial. This is not suitable if you are having money issues because the interest rates will be more erratic. In most cases, when the market is good, you will get a higher interest rate than a regular savings account. These accounts are FDIC insured, so the bank is still liable for lost funds.

Money market accounts have fewer restrictions than regular savings accounts for both the client and the bank. Institutions will have more freedom in how they can use the funds for their portfolios. Remember, though, that the banks are still liable. These accounts also require a higher minimum balance, so make sure you always have the funds you need to avoid major penalties.

Certificate of Deposit:

These are a highly specialized class of savings accounts that are only offered by certain institutions. There are many different types of certificate of deposit (CD) accounts, so talk with your financial institution to determine which one is best for you. These are great for people with a long-term savings plan as they have the potential to yield much higher interest rates. You can use these accounts to build extra wealth until retirement or to save up for major expenses like buying a home. You can get CDs that offer no penalty as well.

529 Plan:

This is specifically a college savings plan that offers financial aid and tax benefits. All states offer some type of plan like this, but you do not have to be a resident of a state to benefit from their particular 529 plan. Anybody can contribute money to this plan. It does not need to be the person who opened it. You can start very early, and by the time your child is ready for school, you will have an immense amount of savings.

When opening this type of account, be mindful of a couple of things:

- This may affect the chances of getting a need's based loan. However, if you plan on having enough money in the account to cover educational costs, that should not matter.
- The funds in these accounts can often only taken out if used towards an educational institution. If your child decides not to go to college, many of these funds may be lost.

IRA:

An IRA, or Individual Retirement Account, is simply a place where you can stash money for retirement. Your account balance is not taxed until you actually withdraw money. This allows you to build up your account with extra interest and not have to worry about it being taxed. Stash away whatever funds you can into an IRA and watch your retirement account build throughout the years. You can set up to where a certain amount from your checking account gets transferred to an IRA every month. An IRA is not like a regular bank account that you can just open anywhere. You will have to go through an investment company or go with a bank that offers it.

Cash at Home:

Let's face it. We are becoming a much more cashless society as time goes on. It is easy to pay for just about anything online, through a credit card, and many other mobile banking options. You can literally touch your smartwatch on a scanner and instantly have your transaction completed. Why would anyone need to carry cash then?

Well, there are still a few options that may require the use of cash. Many wealthy individuals pay for everything in cash because it is easier for them to keep track of their expenses. Also, consider what would happen if the grid goes down. We hate to get into the doom and gloom of things, but it can happen. It's important to have some cash around if it ever does.

When people keep cash in their homes, it is located in various places like wallets, drawers, pocketbooks, under the mattress, or safes. The last option is the best option. While it's not a big deal to have a few bucks here or there left in a drawer, any large amount of cash needs to be kept secure to prevent loss or theft. At any time, your house could be broken into, or suffer through a natural disaster that causes all f your cash to go away. You could easily lose thousands of dollars if your money is not secure.

While the majority of your funds should be placed in a financial institution of some sort, it is important to have a certain amount of cash at home for emergencies. It is recommended that you have enough cash stockpiled for at least two or three days. Determine what that would be for you based on your finances. Remember, we made a budget earlier.

For large sums of cash, it is best to keep it secured in a fireproof and waterproof safe or lockbox. You can get quality safes at reasonable prices. It will be worth it knowing your money is guarded against all sorts of disasters. Buy something that does not look like a safe or lockbox. This will create a diversion for anyone that may see it. Also, keep it in a secure place where no one besides yourself knows where it is. Really, do not allow anyone, unless it is someone you really trust, to know where this safe is. It can be hard to know who is a thief and who is not. You can also buy boxes that are bolted to the floor or just very difficult to move. Do the best you can to keep your money from getting lost.

Different Financial Institutions:

When people think of depositing money, they think of banks. These are certainly the most common types of financial institutions, especially for the general public. However, banks are not your only options. There are various types of institutions where your money can be handled, and we will go over a few of them.

Credit Unions:

The products and services you will receive from a bank versus a credit union are fairly similar. They will both offer a variety of checking and saving accounts, along with loans, and business accounts. The main difference here is that banks are for-profit, while credit unions are non-profit. This can provide both advantages and disadvantages when using a credit union.

Since credit unions are non-profit, they are customer-owned. Once you qualify for a membership, you can take part in this ownership. These institutions often claim better customer service, but they are not as convenient as larger banks due to limited locations. Many credit unions also don't offer things like online service or mobile apps. If you are someone that wants worldwide access in this manner, then you are probably better off going with larger banks.

Some things to consider here are the interest rates and fees. Credit unions generally offer higher interest rates for various accounts and lower fees on loans. If you are okay with the lower amount of accessibility that comes with larger banks, then this may be a good option for you.

Brokerage Firms:

Brokerage firms are places like Charles Schwab or Fidelity Investments. There are dozens of others in the United States. These types of institutions deal strictly with investments and will provide a different option for various investment funds outside of a bank. You will still have to use a bank or credit union for regular accounts. Brokerage companies essentially act as a middle man between buyers and sellers of various investments.

Full-service brokerage accounts provide a full-time financial adviser that will look over all of your investments. Discount brokerages are usually online platforms that allow you to make all of your investments on your own. They will have lower fees but offer much less help compared to a full-service firm.

Insurance

One of the biggest securities you need to protect your finances and prevent your savings from being depleted is having your valuables insured. This includes health, life, car, and home. Insurance is one of those expenses that you will have regularly and may not ever need it. However, if you ever do, you will be very glad you had it. Many people have lost their livelihoods and even gone into major debt because they were not insured properly.

Insurance can be very tricky, so make sure to find a good agent who can help you with this. You should do your best to find great deals on insurance; however, it is not an expense you want to avoid completely. Good insurance can save you in many disastrous situations. We will break down the specific insurance policies you should have in place and why they are important.

Health Insurance:

Medical costs are extremely expensive. Even routine tests and procedures can make a huge dent in someone's pocketbook. Statistically speaking, most families are one medical emergency away from bankruptcy. In reality, it is hard to imagine anyone not being financially ruined by a major illness or accident if they don't have insurance unless they are multi-millionaires. It is important to have good health insurance that will cover all of your needs while having the least amount of copays and other out-of-pocket expenses.

Unfortunately, health insurance costs are not cheap, and the prices will not be going down any time soon. Considering that a single night in a hospital can cost thousands of dollars, even the most minimal policy can be beneficial. At the very least, you will not get the full brunt of medical costs and will hopefully avoid financial ruin. If you are lucky, your insurance will be covered partially by your employer. If not, you may have to look into group plans or buy private insurance.

Auto Insurance:

Most of us need to have a car in order to get around. It is not always practical to walk everywhere or rely on public transportation. Cars come with a lot of expenses. One of them that you cannot go without is auto insurance. First of all, do not buy a car you cannot comfortably afford, and do not get more features than you need. The more features the car has, the higher your insurance rates will be. Take all of this into account.

Auto insurance protects you from damage, injury, theft, and liability. If you get into an accident and it is determined to be your fault, you better have some insurance to cover you. Otherwise, you will be facing some hefty lawsuits. If your car gets damaged, you will have some major repair costs. Even small dents can run a few hundred dollars. Also, there is always a chance your car can be broken into or stolen. Auto insurance will help cover lost items, including your car. Good auto insurance can also help cover damages from personal injury and loss of wages by not being able to work.

Even I nothing happens, if you get pulled over and have no insurance, you will pay heavily in fines. Don't risk it. If you must have a car, do not leave out the car insurance. It will save you immensely in the long run.

Homeowners' Insurance:

Owning your own home is a great luxury to have. You can design it as you please and stock it up with your favorite furniture, artwork, or artifacts. A home is a place you go to at night and feel safe. A home is your castle, so why not protect it the best you can. We are not talking about security systems, which are also important. We are talking about homeowners' insurance. While having your own house is a luxury, insurance to protect it is not. This is an absolute necessity, and if you don't have it, you will pay dearly.

Imagine how much work you put into your home, and then imagine losing it in an instant. What's worse, imagine not being able to rebuild or claim any losses on the home or your personal items. This is a reality if you don't have homeowners' insurance. When you buy a home in the first place, your mortgage company will require you to have this type of insurance. If they find out that you don't, you will be penalized, and the mortgage company will provide you with insurance at a much greater cost. Well, at least it's better than losing everything.

While various insurance policies can be customized to your specific needs, there are a few standard items that must be incorporated. All insurance policies should cover the following, at the very minimum.

- Damage to your interior or exterior due to vandalism, fires, hurricanes, and various other disasters should be covered. Damage from things like earthquakes or floods may need extra coverage.
- Personal items like clothes, jewelry, appliances, or furniture should also be covered from damage due to a natural disaster.
- Personal liability from damage or injuries will be covered. This is to protect you from lawsuits if someone gets injured or has their personal property damaged while on your property. This can include damage done by pets. For example, if your dog bites someone, insurance will pay their medical expenses. Many policies provide a minimum of $100,000 of coverage. Most experts recommend at least $300,000 to be safe.
- If your home is damaged and unlivable, homeowners' insurance will provide you with a temporary house or hotel until everything is fixed. If your home is permanently damaged, insurance will pay off the remaining balance of the loan and give you a check for the amount

you had paid based on what the original value of the home was when you purchased it. For example, if you bought a home for $200,000 and have $150,000 left on the loan, insurance will pay off the $150,000 balance and write you a check for $50,000.
- Insurance will also provide coverage in the event of theft.

Add in the cost of homeowners' insurance before you purchase any type of home. It is something you cannot afford to not have. You will be protecting your home, yourself, and your family.

Life Insurance:

After we pass away, our bills do not stop immediately. It would be nice if they did, but unfortunately, they do not. When someone passes away, their living dependents can face a lot of hardships due to funeral costs, loss of wages, and loss of insurance. When someone is grieving the loss of a loved one, the last thing they should have to worry about is financial matters.

Life insurance is an essential way to make sure your loved ones are provided for even if you pass away. This is extremely important if you are the primary breadwinner in the household. There are different coverage levels available, ranging from $100,000 all the way into the millions. The higher the coverage, the more you will pay. You don't have to make sure your family lives in luxury if you pass away, but you should make sure they have their basic living expenses covered.

When determining your life insurance coverage, calculate your expenses like mortgage, loans, credit cards, utilities, car payments, food, and other miscellaneous items. As you go through life, update your policy as needed. For example, if you move into a new home, adjust your policy coverage amount to account for your new mortgage payment. Your family will face some hardships no matter what if you pass away, however, do your best to reduce their financial burden.

Long-Term Disability Coverage:

This is an insurance type that many people don't pay attention to or think they will need. According to the Social Security Administration, three out of 10 workers will experience an injury and become disabled. This will make them unable to work, which will cause them to lose their wages. Your health insurance will help cover your medical bills, but what about your daily expenses. Hopefully, you will have a nice nest egg saved up, but even this will run out eventually. If you can avoid dipping into your savings, then why not do so?

Disability coverage is essential to make sure your daily expenses are covered in the event you cannot work for weeks, months, years, or even permanently. You may be able to get short-term and long-term disability coverage from work. If so, this may be the best option.

If not, then look at private options. Read all of the fine print to determine how much coverage you will receive and for how long.

Do not think of insurance as an added expense. Think of it as an investment in safeguarding your most important items. Having good insurance coverage will prevent extreme financial hardship, debt, and bankruptcy in the long run. When you invest money in insurance, you save money during major disasters. Seek out a trusted insurance agent and get the best deal you can for yourself. Having good insurance may be expensive, but it will give you a lot of peace of mind.

It's Simple Math

For most individuals, investing was not taught; however, the idea of saving your money was. There are many financial gurus other there that rail against saving because your money is just sitting around not doing anything. Others will say that investing is too risky, and you should save the vast majority of your funds. We are here to say that you can do both.

You don't have to risk all of your money in investments, nor do you have to save all of your money in a bank account. Break it down into percentages. For example, if you save about 10 percent of your income, put half of it into various savings or checking accounts, and invest the other half. Also, the more money you save, the more money you will have to invest. It is simple math. You will also have more room for risks because you will have extra money in case things go wrong. Learn to save your income and then develop the mindset you need to start investing.

Chapter 5: The Time Advantage

We have learned that investing means putting money into something in the hopes of creating a return. For this book, we have been focusing on passive funds, which are some of the safest ways to invest. They still come with a certain amount of risk, and the potential to lose money is still there. This is where the time advantage is crucial. People often wait until they are in their 30s, 40s, and beyond before they even think about investing. While there is nothing wrong with jumping into the investment world later in life, time can really be a disadvantage for you. You will have less time to learn and build wealth for yourself and your family.

Use time to your advantage as it will be a major factor in determining your long-term wealth. If you are able to start investing in your 20s, or even teenage years, then you will really be able to benefit from the time factor. You will have more time to create wealth, more opportunities to take risks, and more ways to invest. The vast majority of investments increase over time on average. The earlier you get into the game, the better your chances will be for success.

The Benefits of Starting Early

Many people do not realize the benefits of starting early when it comes to investments. They feel that they only can when they are financially secure. Unfortunately, for many people, this does not occur until later in life, if at all. Part of becoming an investor is learning to manage wealth better and then working with what you have. This was one of the reasons we went over the importance of saving. The sooner you learn how to save, the sooner you have the money to start investing.

Nowadays, you do not need a lot of capital to get started. Jump in as soon as you can with what you have. There may never be a perfect time to start investing. If your goal is long-term wealth, then this should not be an issue. In fact, when it comes to investing, the objective is to gain wealth over the long run. If you plan on putting money into something hoping for a quick return, then you are not investing, you are gambling. It may be more difficult in some ways to invest at a younger age, but the future benefits heavily outweigh any temporary hardships one will face. We will go over the many positives that come from being timely.

Compound Returns:

The power of compound returns will be extremely beneficial for you in the long run. The rate at which your wealth grows will amaze you. The earlier you start investing, the more time you will have to use compound returns to your advantage. Being able to reinvest your earnings over time will be a great addition to your portfolio. We will cover this concept with more detail in the next chapter.

Risk-Taking:

Even with the safest investments, there is always some risk involved. When you are a young investor, you will have the opportunity to take more risks simply because you will have more years of earning ahead of you. If you make some major financial blunders in your 20s or 30s, it will be easier to recover than if you're in your 50s or 60s. Also, you will likely have fewer people who depend on you at a younger age. Risks can be hard to take when other people may be affected too.

When you start investing at a young age, take a few extra chances once in a while. If it works, it will be a great win. If it doesn't, you will have time to recover. As you approach the later decades of your life, you can opt for safer investments that will get you through the rest of your life. Risks are a part of investing, and the more time you have to take them, the better off you will be.

The Learning Curve Is Greater:

There is a significant learning curve when it comes to investing. You will have plenty of successes and failures along the way. The earlier you begin, the more opportunity you will have to learn for both of these. Over time, you will be able to hone your investment skills and strategies and gain a lot of experience along the way. Getting to know how the market works takes time. Make sure you have as much of it as you need. If you start investing at a later date, you will lack the time it takes to make a well-informed and educated decision. Get in the game early, so you have enough time to learn the techniques.

Improves Spending Habits

It is no secret that children and young adults do not possess the best money management skills. These are something that develops over time with experience and responsibility. Some parents taught their children early about how to manage money, while others never learn. The great thing about investing is that it helps improve your spending habits. Start investing in your 20s, and you will develop great money management skills by the time you're in your 30s and 40s.

When you invest, you learn the value of money and do not take it for granted. Start at a young age, and you are less likely to overstep your financial boundaries in the future. Even when you lose money, you will inevitably learn some lessons along the way, which will make you more financially responsible in the future. In the end, it does not matter how much you make; it matters how much you keep. When you improve your spending habits, you will keep more of what you make.

Better Quality of Life:

Investing at a young age gives you a major head start in the world of personal finances. You will learn to manage money sooner and have more time to build up your wealth. While money does not bring happiness, per se, it can certainly make life easier to live. When you have more money, you have more opportunity to do the things you love like travel, eat out, take up hobbies, or enjoy a night on the town. Furthermore, you can deal with various struggles that come your way much more efficiently. For example, it is easier to maintain your house or car when your finances are more stable. You will have more financial stability throughout adulthood and even after you retire. You will have a greater quality of life because you will live more comfortable and stress-free.

More Time for Recovery

Most good investments will increase in value over time. This does not mean there won't be setbacks along the way. If you hold onto an investment long enough, it will falter at some point. If you start investing early, you will have more time for recovery. A certain investment may take years to recover. If you purchased this investment in your 20s or 30s, you would have less to worry about than if you invested in your 60s.

The bottom line is, you need to start investing in order to have a more stable financial future. Time can be your greatest ally or your worst enemy. Financial goals are achieved through consistent effort and careful planning over the course of time. The good years will balance out the bad years, and you will ultimately be left with good results.

Knowing When You're Ready

We have been reinforcing the fact that you should start investing as soon as you can. We will always stand by this fact. However, you must also know when the right time to invest is. We are not talking about timing the market. We mean determining when the right time to invest is for you based on your circumstances. While there will never be a perfect time to invest, there are a few things you should consider first.

- Do you have extra cash lying in your savings account? If you have very little or no savings, then we do not recommend investing just yet. Work on building up some extra cash first before putting money into investments. While there are risks involved with investing, our intention is not to have you lose everything you have. We want you to have enough money in case of emergencies. At least six to 12 months is the general rule. Once you have enough savings to provide some cushion in your bank account while also investing a good portion, then you are ready to start.
- Determine if the money you have is needed for anything else for the next few years. For example, if you are saving up to buy a house or to get a procedure done, then don't take this money and put it into another investment. You may want to consider a high-yield savings account to build up some extra capital more quickly. If you can spare some cash, then definitely use it for some passive fund investments.

- Evaluate everything in your life and determine what is needed the most. If you did not invest this money, what else could you possibly do with it? If you need it for essentials like food or shelter, then that takes priority. If you have a lot of debt, then try to pay that down first. If there is nothing more important you can be spending that money on, then the best option is to invest.

It is important to have some amount of financial stability before investing. This is why we encourage saving as soon as possible so you can start investing as soon as possible. Do not let anyone else determine what choices you make. Your personal circumstances should dictate when it is the right time to start investing.

Long-Term Investing

The best part about starting off as a young investor is that you will be able to invest for the long haul. If your plan is to play the stocks and try to make a big return quickly, well first, we recommend that you don't do this. Our goal is not to make you Wall Street Millionaires here. Second, there is no time advantage to consider here. If your objective is a quick return, it does not really matter if you do it in your 20s or 60s unless you plan on doing this for several decades and take your chances.

We want to highlight the benefits of long-term investing, which increase drastically on average when started at an earlier age. When it comes to investing for your future, there is a myriad of paths you can take to build a better financial life. Even with the passive investment funds, we have focused on; there is no single path a person has to take. We will go over some advantages that long-term investing has to offer that short-term investors cannot benefit from. Time the market is nearly impossible, but getting into the market at the right time is essential.

- Long-term investing takes almost all of your emotions out of the equation. Major fluctuations in the market, one way or another, will not have you sitting on the edge of your seat, waiting to buy or sell. Sticking with stocks and securities over the long term allows you to focus on the extended gains in the future. This is the meat and potatoes of a long-term investment.
- According to research and data, these types of investment will almost always make you right. While there will be plenty of ups and downs, if you hold onto investments long enough, your portfolio should grow in value. This is another reason to get in as early as you can.
- We here all the time about people becoming millionaires and billionaires in the stock market. This takes a special kind of skill, and very few people can do it. With long-term investments, things become much less complicated, so anyone can do it. Ther are no hassles about learning different trade styles platforms. You will not be an active trader with long-term investing. You simply have to pick

out businesses that are well run and will provide growth for decades. Even if you make mistakes along the way, you will still end up winning in the end.
- Being a long-term investor will help you sleep better at night. You won't have to stay up all night wondering if your stock will plummet. You will be dealing with less volatility.
- Your investment risk drops significantly. With short-term investing, you are attempting to jump in and out constantly and could miss out on major upswings in the market. When you are in it for the long haul, these risk factors go away. You most miss out on big gains when you stick with companies you feel strongly in.
- Commission costs are not a big deal and even an afterthought with long-term investments. The gains you achieve will ultimately cancel out these commission fees.
- Investment mistakes are easy to correct. If you stick with companies that display a winning business model, a large number of mistakes will fix on their own.

Whatever age you have the money to start investing in long-term passive funds, do so. If you are a parent, you may also open an account for your children so they can start learning about money at a young age. This will only be to your benefit. The time advantage is a huge factor in promoting long-term wealth. Make full use of it.

Starting Late

Many people did not have the ability to start investing early for whatever reason. Many people just did not have access to information. While we promote starting your investment journey as soon as possible, it is not too late to get in the game if you are closer to retirement age. You will not have the time advantage as you would when you were younger, but a few changes in strategy can significantly improve your financial well-being. Once people are in their 50s and 60s, their main goal usually becomes saving for retirement. This was they can enjoy several years of good living without worrying about having an income. We will go over a few tips for those of you getting a late start on retirement savings.

- First of all, you need to accelerate your savings amount. You can do this by contributing more money to an employee-sponsored retirement account, like a 401(k). If your employer does not offer this, or if you're self-employed, then you can always open a private account like an IRA through your bank.
- You can also start downsizing by getting rid of items you no longer want or need. Some individuals even downsize their cars and homes. This can provide a lot of savings by reducing monthly payments. Once you downsize, you can use this extra money to put into a high-yield account like a CD, or one of your retirement account. Even a regular savings account is better than nothing, but we want to make your money work for you the best way possible.

- Avoid buying luxuries you don't need so you can avoid extra debt. For example, if your car is still working fine, then don't buy a new one until you need it. Once again, you can use the money you save to put into your various accounts.
- Keep your investment portfolio on the low-risk side. A fund with a high percentage of bonds can still bring in some extra income. Of course, investors recommend a mix of stocks and bonds for maximum gain and limited risk. Keep less of your assets in cash so you can grow more of your money. Beyond what you need for emergencies and daily costs, keep your money out of regular bank accounts.
- Avoid experimenting with trades or investment vehicles you do not understand. Keep the risk level dialed down the older you get. You can experiment with riskier investments when you are young, but when you are closer to retirement, keep it safe, and grow your income the best you can.

The bottom line is, start investing as soon as you can. If you are reading this book in your 50s, then start investing in your 50s. Don't read this book, and then forget about it for ten years. The quicker you start, the more comfortable you will feel.

Chapter 6: The Miracle of Compound Interest

We touched on the idea of compound interest in the previous chapter. We will get into more detail about it here, including the miracle it can have on your financial future. The simplest way to explain this concept is to call it "interest on interest." It makes the interest grow at an increased rate. With compound interest, the interest is calculated on the accumulated interest over time in addition to the original principal amount. This can create a snowball effect since the initial investment and the income earned from those investments grow together.

The benefits of compound interest increase exponentially with the more time we have for the investment to grow. This takes us back to the point we made in the previous chapter: start early! If you have 50 years of compound interest with the same investment, versus 30 years, then mathematically speaking, you will have earned much more money over a 50-year period.

Let's do a quick calculation to show the effects. If you saved $50 a month for ten years and had no interest earned, you would end up with $6,000. If you earned eight percent interest every year on your investment, you would end up with $9,150 after ten years. What a difference this can make. Now imagine investing $100 or $200. The money earned on compound interest alone at this rate would increase your money by 50%.

For your information, $200 invested monthly over ten years at eight percent interest would give you $36,000 if you never take anything out and only make deposits.

To help you understand further the benefit of compound interest, we will compare it to simple interest. Simple interest can also be beneficial on a smaller scale, but will not provide anywhere near the returns of compound interest. This is especially true for long-term investments. Let's say that you invested $5,000 dollars into an account. This is your principal amount to start off with. With simple interest, you would earn interest on that $5,000 for as long as it is in the account, but not any extra interest on the interest you have earned. Essentially, the interest earned does not get added to your initial investment to increase the principal amount.

With compound interest, the interest you earn gets added to your principal balance, which you will then earn further interest on. For example, if the initial investment was $5,000, and by the end of the first month you have $5,008, then $5,008 is your new principal balance, which you will earn interest on. Compound interest benefits will make a huge difference as the years go by.

If you want to reap the amazing benefits of compound interest, then you must be ready to invest your money into accounts that offer it. Once you place your funds into these accounts, it is important to add in more money when you can and avoid taking anything out for as long as possible. Once you start seeing the interest earnings stacking up in your account, it will be hard not to let it keep going. Earning money can become addictive at some point.

Investment Accounts for Earning Compound Interest

It is important to choose specific accounts that will offer compound interest to help build up your wealth over time. Imagine watching our money grow while it's just sitting there in a bank. This is what the miracle of compound interest is all about. There are numerous banking and investment accounts; we will go over that allow you to benefit from this type of growth.

Bank Investments:

Cds and money market investments frequently offer compound interest growth options. Many banking institutions will compound on a daily basis, even if you don't see it occurring on a daily basis. You may only see the payout once a month or how often the bank chooses to do so. The goal here is to let your money sit in the same account, so it continues to compound over time. Choose accounts that have the highest interest rates, and you will enjoy even better benefits. The growth you see year after year will astound you.

Zero-Coupon Bond:

With a traditional bond, you will receive frequently receive interest payments, but they do not compound. When you open a zero-coupon bond, you will purchase it for a fraction of the initial value. Through compounding, it will ultimately reach its value price once it matures. With this option, you are saving a lot of money on your initial investment and will reap the rewards later on.

Compound Earnings by Reinvestment:

This will take a little bit of technique. When you open a mutual fund, you will earn dividends from your stock investments. These dividends simply sit in your account as they accumulate. To make them work more productively, you can reinvest these dividends to earn even more dividends.

Some mutual fund and stock options have their own dividend reinvestment plans that automatically buy more of the stocks or funds. Other options require your input. This means that you can pick where and when to reinvest your money. By following this strategy, you can turn almost any investment account into a compounding account to make your money work for you as much as possible.

Treasury Bills:

Treasury bills are fully backed by the treasury department. They are short-term government debt used to fulfill various projects and financial obligations. They are considered a safe investment.

These bills are purchased at face value, and when they mature, the investors will receive full value for them. It is recommended to hold onto these bills until full maturity is obtained; otherwise, you are risking a loss. Basically, before purchasing, make sure you do not need the money for anything else. It varies on how fast these treasury bills will mature.

The Ugly Side

We have been speaking about the miracle of compound interest. When it comes to savings and investment accounts, it is definitely a great benefit to have. You can earn exceptional amounts of money, and if you are starting late in the game, accounts that offer compound interest are a great thing to have in your portfolio. While compound interest is great when you are talking about saving, there is an ugly side to it, and that is when it comes to loans.

We will refer back to the number 5,000. Imagine for a minute, having a $5,000 outstanding balance on a loan with compound interest. If this loan has a 15% annual percentage rate while also compounding daily, you will owe $5,063.70 after one month. If you put in $100, it will go down to $4,963.70, but then will go back up over $5,000 by the end of the next month. Imagine how long it will take to pay this loan off and how much extra money you will be spending by the time you are done. To give you a hint, it will be a lot more than $5,000.

This is why people hold onto their loans for almost all of their adult lives. Student loans, credit cards, and mortgages are some of the largest debts that people carry and can almost never get away from. Interest rates can crush someone's finances, so you want to be very careful when you take out a loan for almost anything. Determine what your monthly rate will be and how long it will take to pay off a loan with specific monthly payments. For example, if you take out a loan for $5,000, determine how long it will take to pay off if you put in $200 a month. Definitely avoid compound interest on loans if you can.

Chapter 7: Portfolio Models

We have now discussed passive investment funds and other various investment topics in great detail. The most important lessons to remember are starting early, focusing on long-term gains, and diversifying your assets. We will get into more details about the last one here as we discuss portfolio models and the benefits they provide.

Investors have various expectations when it comes to their money and where it goes. They may seek high returns, low risk, tax-efficiency, or a combination of all of these when building up their investments. This is where we get to portfolio models, or model portfolios, which can provide all of these benefits and more if created properly. Model portfolios are a diversified group of assets designed to achieve a return with a low amount of risk. There are a variety of portfolios that an investment manager or financial adviser can come up with that will be geared towards your financial objectives for the future. Model portfolios allow investors to use effective investment methods with very minimal management effort.

The diversification strategy utilized with these investment portfolios helps reduce risk by distributing your funds throughout numerous financial vehicles, asset categories, and industries. Your money will never be in the same spot. This technique still allows for decent returns while also reducing the risk that comes with short-term and singular investments. When financial advisers are creating a portfolio model, they will often pick investments that may react in different ways when similar events occur. A perfect example of this is holding shares in railroad stocks and airline stocks. If railroad workers go on strike, it will cause the shares of railroad stock to decline immensely. However, since people are no longer taking trains, they may start flying much more, so the airline stock will go up. This is just a hypothetical example to show you how it works.

The above example of the railroad and airline stock could create another issue. Since they are both parts of the travel industry, both stock prices could take a hit. This is why you cannot just diversify within a single industry, either. You have to really invest across the board. For example, you can hold stock and securities in the travel industry, along with the food and clothing industry.

The great thing about model portfolios is that they were designed by industry professionals and experts. When a financial expert is working with you on your portfolio, they will use their professional analysis and detailed research to develop an ideal investment strategy for you. After this, they will pick specific assets to build your portfolio. During all of this, they will have put in a clear review process to help assess each individual investment in the portfolio and will monitor the performance on a regular basis. Basically, your model portfolio will be built and overseen by a professional in the financial field. This way, you can follow and assess the investments from time to time and allow the expert to run the day-to-day operations.

Do your research and make sure to go with an established financial adviser.

Model portfolios have to meet specific benchmarks and perform at an acceptable level. Financial advisers will rebalance your investments when needed. This means they will constantly monitor your investments, and if alterations are needed, they will readjust the percentages of each asset in the portfolio. This rebalancing process includes buying and selling off assets to maintain asset allocation. By doing this, they can ensure you are maximizing your profits and minimizing your risks. Imagine how much work this would be if you were picking each individual stock on their own without anyone's help. Most people do not have the time or desire to be professional investors. This is why managed portfolio models become a blessing.

While there are many positive attributes to a model portfolio, there are disadvantages too. When you commit to a portfolio of this kind, you lose control of your asset management. Your financial adviser will have full control of your money that is in this portfolio. If you have a great financial adviser, then it's not a big deal. However, this can make a lot of people uncomfortable. People are used to having complete access to their funds at all times, and this route takes that access away from them. Like we said before, do your research before picking a financial adviser or investment company.

When you put your money in a regular bank account, they are FDIC insured. This means you will not lose the money you put in due to mismanagement by the bank. What you put in is what you get out, plus interest. With investments, including model portfolios, performance is not guaranteed, which means you could end up with less money than you put in. Even the best money managers can lose money during a descending market. Of course, if your plan is for the longterm, you should not worry too much about this one. Eventually, your portfolio value will go up.

Finally, before you sign up for a model portfolio, understand the fees that you will incur. The portfolios will be managed by a financial expert, which means you will have to pay them for their time and effort. It is certainly worth it because managing these portfolios would be a daunting task if you did it alone. However, make sure they are not gouging you with excessive fees. It may behoove to compare multiple advisers to get an average. In the end, if your investment portfolio is bringing in maximum returns, then these fees may become a non-issue.

Model Portfolio Examples

While the financial adviser or investment company will be doing the majority of the heavy lifting for you, you must still understand the basics of a model portfolio and what makes them successful. If you do not, they may run you through the wringer without you even realizing it. Imagine how you would feel if you invested your hard-earned money, only to find it all gone. The chances of this happening are slim to none, but we still do not want you to become a statistic. We will go over some model portfolio examples that experts in the industry have created for themselves. You don't have to follow these examples. They are just here to give you an idea.

The 90/10 Portfolio by Warren Buffett:

This model is broken down into 90% S&P tracker funds (a type of ETF), and 10% short-term government bonds. Mr. Buffett feels this type of investment is good for those who are not experienced investors. This path steers clear of expenses and high fees. Critics of this model cite that the portfolio investments are exclusive to the U.S. and devoid of any international companies. This can limit diversification that comes from the international front. This simple portfolio model has performed well over many decades. If it is accepted by the world's most successful investor, then it is definitely something to look at.

Ultimate Byu and HoldStrategy byPaulMerriman

This particular portfolio by successful investor Paul Merriman is stock exclusive. He does believe in holding stocks, too. This model has a range of different stock holdings, and each one makes up 10 percent of the portfolio. The following are the investments that he holds:

- 10% S&P 500
- 10% U.S. Large Cap Value
- 10% U.S. Small Cap Blend
- 10% U.S. Small Cap Value
- 10% U.S. REITs
- 10% International Large Cap Blend
- 10% International Large Cap Value
- 10% International Small Cap Blend
- 10% International Small Cap Value
- 10% Emerging Markets

Mr. Merriman's strategy is to use the S&P 500 as a base to start out with and then add small amounts of various other assets to help reduce risk. This is a highly diverse stock portfolio.

Ivy League Endowments:

When you translate the various investments of Ivy League endowments, like Yale or Harvard, into ETF-based asset classes, they are much more accessible to the general public. These endowments can be hard to replicate when done on their own. Here is a breakdown of this investment portfolio.

- 35% U.S. Equity
- 28% Bonds
- 15% Foreign Equity
- 11% Commodities
- 11% Real Estate

No Brainer Portfolio by Bill Bernstein

This is a relatively simple portfolio model created by intelligent asset allocator, Bill Bernstein. He proposes an equal share of all the assets involved within the portfolio.

- 25% Bonds
- 25% S&P 500
- 25% U.S. small-cap stocks
- 25% European stocks

Each individual portfolio model has its strengths and weaknesses and is developed based on the goals of an individual investor. Your personal models may look similar to, or be completely different from the ones above. Whatever the case, go in the direction that is right for you.

Steps to Building a Profitable Portfolio

In the end, your main goal in building a portfolio is to make it profitable. You expect to put a certain amount of money in, and then have a much greater amount when you reach the end of the road. As long as you've achieved that, you have been successful. Investors can follow a systematic approach to construct a portfolio that is geared towards their investment goals. We will go over the steps of this systematic approach.

Determine Your Appropriate Asset Allocation:

Assessing your individual financial situation and long-term objectives are the first step in constructing your portfolio. You must look at your age and how much time you have to grow your investments. Also, determine how much capital you have to make an investment. A new college graduate in their 20s would have a different approach to building a portfolio than a 50-year-old who's providing for a family.

You must also factor in your personality and tolerance for taking risks. Some people are much more comfortable with taking risks and are also more aggressive in their approach. This individual should consider a different strategy than someone who is more conservative. Even with safer investments like passive funds, you can increase your income potential by increase the risk level behind your assets. An aggressive portfolio would have more equities like stocks, and less fixed-income securities like bonds. A conservative portfolio would be the opposite. If aggressive portfolios cause you to not sleep well at night, then these riskier investments may not be your forte. It will not be worth the stress.

For the sake of profitability, there is something known as the risk/return tradeoff. Take as much risk as you feel comfortable, and don't get rid of the risk completely; otherwise, you will have no returns. If this is the case, you might as well stick with a regular savings or money market account. Once you have determined what assets you want to focus on, then you can move on to step 2.

Achieving the Portfolio:

For this step, you need to divide your capital between the appropriate asset classes. This is pretty easy on the basic level as you can simply separate stocks and bonds. You can further breakdown the asset classes into smaller subclasses. An investor may divide equity allocations between various industries and also foreign versus domestic stocks. Bonds can be divided between short-term versus long-term and government versus corporate. There are various paths you can take to fulfill your asset allocation strategy. Here are a few things to consider.

- If picking stocks, chose the ones that satisfy your level of risk. Your financial adviser can help you make the decisions by doing an analysis of the opportunities and the risks involved. While your adviser will be handing the daily tasks, stay abreast of all the companies in your portfolio, and follow market trends so you can be informed too. Also, stay current on all industry news. It is still your money, after all.
- When picking bonds, look into the bond type, credit rating, and general interest rate environment.
- Mutual funds allow you to hold stocks and bonds that are professionally researched and picked for you. These funds are more aggressively managed, so they have higher fees to pay to the fund manager. Index funds are a passive option that has fewer fees.

Reassessing Portfolio Weights:

By this step, you should have an established portfolio. Congratulations on taking a positive investment step. Once this occurs, you are not done. Many people open accounts like these and then forget about them. While the fund manager will be looking over your account and rebalancing as needed, it is important for you to remain informed about what adjustments are occurring.

You may have life changes that occur over time. For example, you may become more educated on various securities, so you are more willing to take risks. At this time, you can shift over to a more aggressive portfolio. Also, if your income increases, you may be able to contribute more money. Your portfolio model is not final at any point. It can be changed as needed.

Rebalancing Strategically:

After assessing your portfolio and determining which securities you want to reduce, decide now which securities you will buy. After making this determination, use the proceeds from the overweighted securities to buy te underweighted ones. Before selling certain stocks, also consider the potential for capital gains taxes. To avoid these, you may simply stop contributing to these overweighted stocks and focus on the underweighted ones. This is definitely a balancing act.

The main focus as you build and rebuild your portfolio is to maintain diversifications. Never allow your funds to become too lopsided in one direction. You must own securities throughout different asset classes, and also own multiple securities within an asset class. This is how you develop the ultimate diversified portfolio. Good luck with creating your personalized portfolio model.

Protecting Your Portfolio

While portfolios are a relatively safe option for new investors who want long-term growth, there are a few extra ways to protect your assets. We have already discussed diversification, which is a major safeguard against losing your investment. Beyond this, there are several other common strategies that you can use to protect your portfolio model.

Non-correlating Assets:

This is a strategy where you hold assets that do not correlate with one another. This means that they react differently to specific market conditions. For example, real estate, bonds, commodities, and currencies will often have inverse relationships with stocks. So when stocks go down, the other assets will go up. This will help keep the volatility of the overall portfolio low.

Stop Losses:

These will help protect your portfolio against falling share prices. There are different types of stops you can use. With a hard stop, you can trigger the sale of a stock by putting a fixed-price on it. This means that if the share price drops to a certain level, the stock will automatically sell. For example, if you bought into a company at $20 a share with a hard stop of $18, the stock will sell automatically if the price drops below $18 a share.

Another type of stop loss is a trailing stop. These are based on percentages rather than hard numbers. This means that if share prices drop a certain percentage, then the stock will automatically sell. For example, we can set our trailing stop at 10%. As share prices go up, the sell value will also go up. If we buy the original shares at $20 each, the stock will automatically sell if it drops below $18 a share, which is a 10% drop. If the share prices rise to $25, then the new sell-off limit will be a 10% drop from this point, which will be $22.50 a share.

Investors who promote stop losses do so because they protect an individual from a rapidly changing market. It can certainly prevent your stock's value from getting too low. Opponents of stop losses state that temporary losses become permanent, and you will miss out on a lot of growth opportunities if the stock rebounds. Both of these facts hold true, and you can decide for yourself if it's a safeguard you want to put in.

Your portfolio will inevitably experience volatility as different investments go up and down. The goal of these protective measures is to shield your assets from this volatility. You can use some or all of them. Bear in mind, the more safeguards you put in, the less chance you have for long-term growth. The key is to find a balance between safety and risk.

As we took you step-by-step through the various passive fund investment strategies, we hope that we opened your eyes to many different ways of building wealth that you never thought of. The days of the past, where a family could rely on a single income, are becoming fewer and far between. It is imperative to learn new methods of increasing wealth. These portfolio models will cap off what you need to provide yourself with safe, passive investment funds.

Conclusion

Thank you for making it through to the end of *A Beginners Guide to Passive Funds*, let's hope it was informative and able to provide you with all of the tools you need to achieve your goals whatever they may be. The idea of money is fascinating, while the thought of losing it is terrifying. While we try not to worship money or finances, it is an entity that makes the world go around. You simply cannot survive without money, so it is best to use it to your advantage. For this to occur, you must approach it in a different manner. You must get rid of your old thoughts and beliefs about how money works, so you can open yourself up to a new realm of possibilities.

Throughout this book, we focused on the idea of investing, which is foreign to a lot of people. Investing is certainly not something that is taught in schools, and many parents do not focus on it. This is because it was never taught to them. If children were lucky, they were at least taught how to save. While saving is better than spending everything, it severely limits your options as far as building your wealth. This is why we delved into the world of investing and showed all of you that it is not as complicated as it may seem.

There are many investment options out there, but we chose to focus on passive investment funds because of their low-risk approach. It is simple for a new investor to get involved with passive funds so they can start building a more productive financial future for themselves. Of course, the concept of easy and low-risk investments does not sit well with many people. The reason for this is the lack of exposure. They have developed a limiting mindset that prevents them from looking outside the box. The first thing any person must do before entering the investment world is to alter their financial mentality. We have provided several techniques on how to do this. Once the mindset shift occurs, then we can start embracing the various investments that are at our disposal. Once again, our focus was passive funds used for long-term growth.

Our objective for this book was to get you comfortable and knowledgeable with passive investment funds so that you can ease into the world of investing without too much anxiety. We also went over ways to increase your savings, which will increase your ability to invest by having more available capital. We also went over strategies to maximize your profits while keeping your risk levels low. Finally, we detailed how you can develop your own portfolio model to bring you long-term wealth until you are ready to retire.

The next step is to take the information from this book and start searching for ways to open up various passive investment fund accounts. This book is really just the starting point. Once you are comfortable with the topics we discussed throughout the previous chapters, then you can move on and learn about many other investment opportunities, including more active and aggressive options. This is only if you choose to, though. This book will serve as your launching pad to great investment success. If you decide to go no further than the information provided here, you will have still taken some significant steps that will impact your financial future. However, if you are a young investor with plenty of time, then we encourage you to keep learning.

We hope this book was informative and opened your eyes to a new world of finance. It can be scary at first, but you must take that first step to make real changes in your life. Take your time, and do not move faster than you feel comfortable.

Finally, if you found this book useful in any way, a review on Amazon is always appreciated! The more people that know about this book, the more people we can help with their financial situation.